THE GOLDEN YEARS OF RAILROADING

HEART OF THE PENNSYLVANIA RAILROAD

The Main Line: Philadelphia to Pittsburgh

ROBERT S. McGONIGAL

© 1996 by Kalmbach Publishing Co. All rights reserved. This book may not be reproduced in part or in whole without written permission of the publisher, except in the case of brief quotations used in reviews. Published by Kalmbach Publishing Co., 21027 Crossroads Circle, P. O. Box 1612, Waukesha, WI 53187.

Printed in the United States of America

Book design: Kristi Ludwig
Series editor: George Drury
Copy editor: Mary Algozin
Division maps: John Signor

On the cover: K4s 3888 assists the two E7 diesels assigned to train 25 up the east slope of the Allegheny Mountains at Bennington Curve, a few miles west of the Pennsylvania Railroad's famous Horseshoe Curve. Photo by Fred McLeod, October 1949.

Publisher's Cataloging in Publication
(Prepared by Quality Books Inc.)

McGonigal, Robert S.
    Heart of the Pennsylvania Railroad : The Main Line : Philadelphia-Pittsburgh / Robert S. McGonigal.
    p.   cm. — (Golden years of railroading ; 4)
    Includes bibliographical references and index.
    ISBN 0-89024-275-5

    1. Railroads—Pennsylvania—History—Pictorial works. 2. Pennsylvania Railroad—History.   I. Title.

TF20.M34 1996   625.1'009'748
                                             QBI96-40083

Contents

Brief history of the Pennsylvania Railroad 5

Philadelphia Terminal and Philadelphia Division 11

Middle Division 45

Pittsburgh Division 81

The Main Line today 125

Index 127

K4s 3888 assists the two E7 diesels assigned to train 25 up the east slope of the Allegheny Mountains at Bennington Curve, a few miles west of the Pennsylvania Railroad's famous Horseshoe Curve. Photo by Fred McLeod, October 1949.

Pennsylvania Railroad

The Pennsylvania Railroad was the dominant member of the American railroad family during its heyday. In an era when there were more than 130 Class 1 railroads, the PRR moved 10 percent of America's freight and 20 percent of its passengers. Its 10,500-mile system served 13 states in the most populous and industrialized region of the country. While its chief rival in the New York-Chicago-St. Louis area — the New York Central — had a small edge in route miles and geographic extent, the Pennsy had greater freight revenues and moved half again as many passengers. Yet despite the vast scale of the PRR's empire, its heart was always the segment from its headquarters city of Philadelphia to the industrial cornucopia of Pittsburgh.

Philadelphians began to notice that the Erie Canal and the National Road (and later the Baltimore & Ohio Railroad) were funneling to New York and Baltimore commerce that might have come to their city and sought to create a transportation system to the west. In 1828 the Main Line of Public Works was chartered to build a railroad and canal linking Philadelphia with the Ohio River. Although rail had not yet eclipsed water transport as the preferred overland mode, the Allegheny Mountains to the west and the undulating country between Philadelphia and the Susquehanna River made water transport impractical for the whole system. Instead, the Main Line would consist of one railroad from Philadelphia to Columbia, another across the mountains, and canals from Columbia and Pittsburgh to the base of the mountains.

By 1832 canals were open from Columbia to Hollidaysburg and from Pittsburgh to Johnstown; in 1834 the Philadelphia & Columbia Railroad began service between its namesake cities, and the Allegheny Portage Railroad was opened over the Alleghenies. The latter was a series of ten rope-operated inclined planes; canal boats were designed to be taken apart and hauled over the mountains. The system was ingenious but inefficient.

The B&O requested a charter for a line to Pittsburgh in 1843. The B&O line was chartered — but so was the Pennsylvania Railroad, on April 13, 1846. Backed by the Philadelphia business community, the new company would build a line from Harrisburg to Pittsburgh. The B&O's charter would be valid only if the PRR were not constructed.

J. Edgar Thomson, who had built the Georgia Railroad, surveyed the route. Although some had advised a line with a steady grade from Harrisburg to the Allegheny summit, he laid out instead a nearly water-level line along the Susquehanna and Juniata rivers from Harrisburg to Altoona, where a steeper grade began for a comparatively short assault on the mountains. This concentrated the problems of a mountain railroad in one area.

Construction began in 1847. Two years later an operating contract with the Harrisburg, Portsmouth, Mountjoy & Lancaster linked the PRR at the state capital with the Philadelphia & Columbia at Lancaster. By 1852 rails ran from Philadelphia to Pittsburgh, via a connection with the Allegheny Portage Railroad between Hollidaysburg and Johnstown. The summit tunnel at Gallitzin, opened in February 1854, bypassed the inclines and created a continuous railroad from Harrisburg to Pittsburgh. (In an early illustration of the Pennsy's penchant for multiple track, more than half the line had been double-tracked by this point.) In 1857 the PRR bought the Main Line of Public Works — including the New Portage Railroad, a Hollidaysburg-Gallitzin replacement for the inclines that was built about the same time as PRR's own line — and in 1861 leased the HPM&L, putting the whole Philadelphia-Pittsburgh line under one management.

Following his tenure as PRR's first chief engineer, J. Edgar Thomson became the road's third president, and his administration from 1852 to 1874 saw an expansion of the company, mostly by leasing or purchasing other railroads, during which it attained nearly its full geographical limits.

Expansion to Chicago and St. Louis

In 1856 three lines west of Pittsburgh were consolidated as the Pittsburgh, Fort Wayne & Chicago Rail Road. PRR held a partial interest in the line. Two years later, the PFtW&C linked up with the PRR in Pittsburgh and completed its line into Chicago. In 1860 the Fort Wayne leased the Cleveland & Pittsburgh, a line from Cleveland through Alliance (where it crossed the Fort Wayne) to the Ohio River and upstream to Rochester, Pennsylvania, where it again met the Fort Wayne.

In 1869 the Pennsy leased the Fort Wayne in a deal that also included the Grand Rapids & Indiana, a line from Richmond, Indiana, north to Fort Wayne and Grand Rapids, Michigan. In 1873 the PRR assembled a route into Toledo; some 50 years later it reached Detroit.

Also west of Pittsburgh lay a string of railroads that formed a route through Columbus to Cincinnati. One was sold at foreclosure and a new company, the Panhandle Railway (named for its passage through the panhandle of West Virginia between Pennsylvania and the Ohio River), took over in 1868. PRR consolidated the Panhandle and a neighboring road as the Pittsburg, Cincinnati & St. Louis Railway, but the name "Panhandle" stuck with it and its successors.

West of Columbus the Columbus, Chicago & Indiana Central Railway had lines to Indianapolis and Chicago. In 1869 the Pennsy leased the CC&IC. Beyond Indianapolis lay the Terre Haute & Indianapolis, which leased the St. Louis, Vandalia & Terre Haute upon its completion in 1870. The TH&I then made traffic agreements with the Panhandle and the CC&IC.

In 1890 the Pittsburg, Cincinnati & St. Louis and several other lines were consolidated as the Pittsburgh, Cincinnati, Chicago & St. Louis Railway, and in 1905 the Vandalia Railroad was incorporated to consolidate the lines west of Indianapolis. The PCC&StL, the Vandalia, and several others were consolidated in 1916 as the Pittsburgh, Cincinnati, Chicago & St. Louis Railroad. In 1921 the PCC&StL was leased to the Pennsylvania.

With the leases of 1869 the PRR suddenly had more than 3,000 miles of line west of Pittsburgh. Rather than try to manage it all from Philadelphia, the PRR organized the Pennsylvania Company to hold and manage the "Lines West." The division of the system into more or less autonomous segments was not altogether successful, partly because the pieces came together at Pittsburgh, where yards and terminals were under separate managements. World War I traffic brought the inefficiencies into sharp focus, and the east-west separation was ended in 1920.

Eastern acquisitions

In 1860 PRR acquired interests in the Cumberland Valley Railroad from Harrisburg to Hagerstown, Maryland, and the Northern Central Railway from Baltimore through Harrisburg to Sunbury, Pennsylvania. Pennsy expanded into the northwestern portion of its native state by acquiring an interest in the Philadelphia & Erie Railroad in 1862 and helping that road complete its line from Sunbury to Erie. A portion of that line came to serve as part of a freight route with easy grades. The rest of the freight route was the Allegheny Valley Railroad, conceived as a feeder from Pittsburgh to the New York Central and the Erie railroads. PRR obtained control of the AV and in 1874 opened a low-grade Harrisburg-Pittsburgh route to the north of the Main Line via the valleys of the Susquehanna and the Allegheny rivers.

Although it was a Philadelphia company, the PRR could not ignore the growing city and port of New York. In 1871 PRR leased several New Jersey rail and canal companies, acquiring lines northeast to Jersey City (where ferries provided a link to New York), south to Cape May, and north along the Delaware River to Belvidere.

To reach Washington, D.C., the Pennsy bought the dormant charter of the Baltimore & Potomac and built a branch from the B&P at Bowie to Washington, which opened in 1872. Congress authorized the PRR to extend its line through Washington to connect with railroads in Virginia.

A direct Philadelphia-Baltimore route was established by means of the Philadelphia, Wilmington & Baltimore. PRR began through service between Jersey City and Washington via the PW&B and the B&P in 1873. The PW&B also included lines down the Delmarva Peninsula that were later extended under PRR auspices to Cape Charles, Virginia.

Consolidation and refinement

From 1880 until 1906, George B. Roberts and Alexander J. Cassatt, PRR's fifth and seventh presidents, respectively, shifted the road's emphasis from expansion to consolidation and refinement. In the 1880s the Pennsy acquired lines from Philadelphia east across New Jersey to the shore and constructed lines up the Schuylkill River into Reading territory. (The West Jersey & Seashore, as the New Jersey lines were known, was combined with the Reading's parallel Atlantic City Railroad in 1933 to form the Pennsylvania-Reading Seashore Lines.) In 1902 the PW&B and the B&P were consolidated as the Philadelphia, Baltimore & Washington Railroad. PB&W and B&O

together formed the Washington Terminal Co., which constructed a new Union Station in Washington that opened in 1907. The PB&W was leased to the PRR in 1917.

Other major additions were extension of the GR&I north to Mackinaw City, Michigan (1882); construction of the Trenton Cutoff, a freight line bypassing Philadelphia (1892); and acquisition of the Western New York & Pennsylvania Railroad, which reached Buffalo and Rochester, New York.

PRR had long been at a competitive disadvantage for New York passenger traffic to the New York Central, which had a terminal, Grand Central, on Manhattan Island. PRR's acquisition of the Long Island Rail Road in 1900 gave impetus to its desire for rail access to Manhattan. After studying proposals for bridges and tunnels, PRR began construction in 1904 of Pennsylvania Station in midtown Manhattan, two tunnels under the Hudson River, four tunnels under the East River, and a double-track line across the Jersey Meadows to connect it to the main line to Philadelphia east of Newark — all electrified with a third-rail system. Penn Station opened in 1910.

By this time the Pennsylvania had achieved full growth, and nearly everywhere it went it was the dominant railroad. In addition, the preceding quarter century had seen the construction of many new freight and passenger facilities, the straightening and widening of most main lines, and the building of many flying junctions and sturdy stone-arch bridges across the system.

Standard, then decline

As the industry leader at the turn of the century, PRR took to calling itself "The Standard Railroad of America," then broadened the slogan to include "the World." In the 20th century, the standardization was largely internal. Though PRR had 6,152 locomotives in 1929, a relative handful of types dominated the roster. Much of Pennsy's standardization was counter to most North American practice: Belpaire boilers on steam engines, position-light signals, electrification of main lines, a numbering system that only belatedly grouped locomotives of the same class, Tuscan red for passenger cars instead of dark green.

During World War II Pennsy's freight traffic doubled and passenger traffic quadrupled. After the war PRR had the same experiences as many other railroads but seemed slower to react, even considering the regulatory burdens then in place, under which all railroads labored. Pennsy was slower to dieselize, and when it did so it bought from every manufacturer. As freight and passengers left for the highways, PRR found itself with too much fixed plant, and it was slow to take up excess trackage or install Centralized Traffic Control. PRR was saddled with a heavy passenger business; it had extensive commuter services centered on New York, Philadelphia, and Pittsburgh, and lesser ones at Chicago, Washington, Baltimore, and Camden, New Jersey. It had gone through the Depression without going bankrupt, and so was never relieved of old debt obligations. PRR did maintain, though, the longest history of dividend payment in U.S. business history.

In 1957, the PRR and NYC, by then troubled twin giants more than rivals, announced plans to merge. Penn Central began operation on February 1, 1968, and became the country's largest

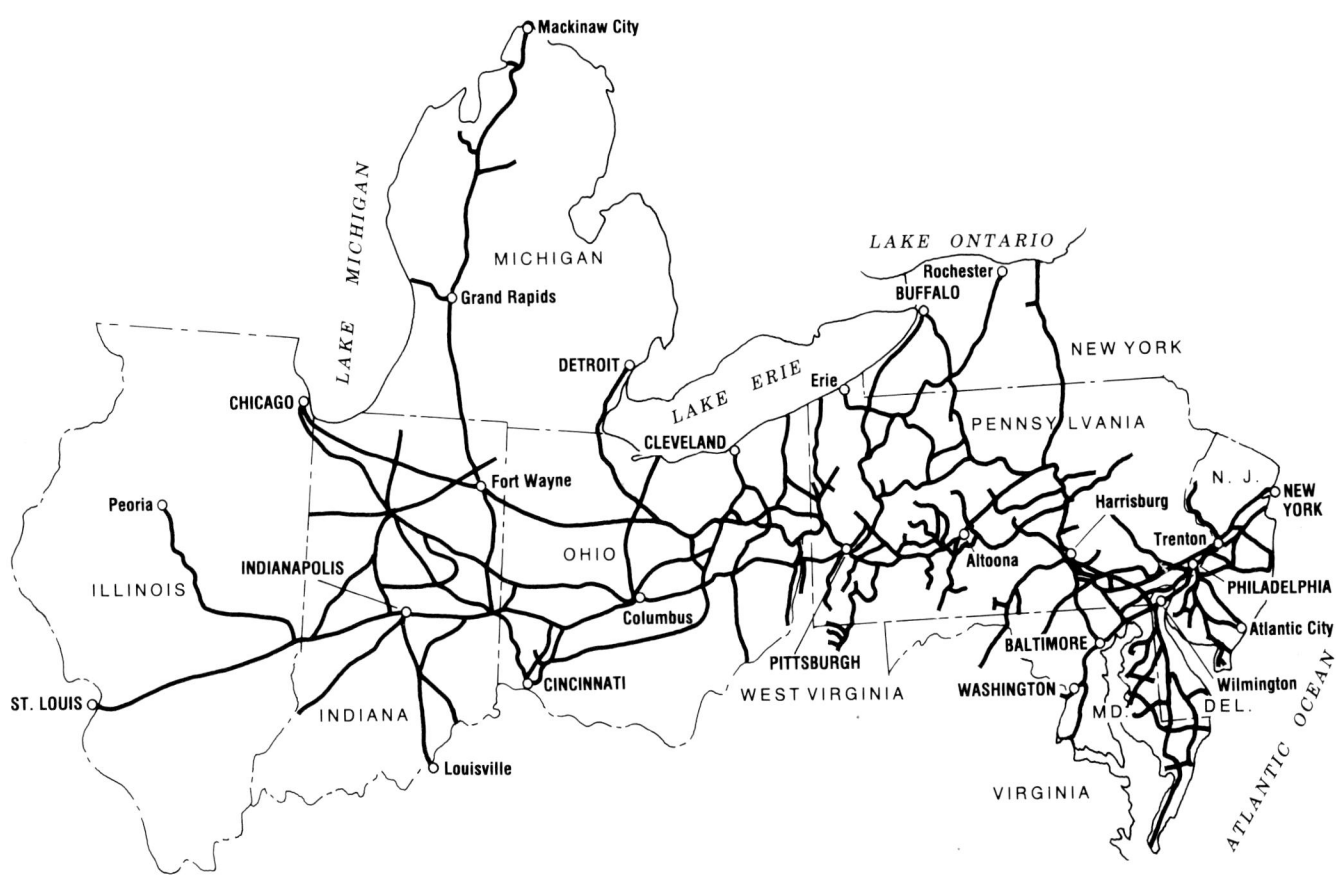

bankruptcy on June 21, 1970. That led to the formation of Conrail, which took over seven bankrupt railroads on April 1, 1976, and became profitable in 1981.

Until PRR restructured its 20 operating divisions into nine regions in 1955, the Philadelphia-Pittsburgh Main Line was composed of four divisions. In addition to other lines in and around PRR's headquarters city, the Philadelphia Terminal Division covered the Main Line from center city to just west of Paoli. The Philadelphia Division encompassed the territory beyond to Marysville, across the Rockville Bridge from Harrisburg. The Middle Division extended from Marysville to the west side of Altoona. The Pittsburgh Division's main stem was Altoona-Pittsburgh. Our look at the Main Line in the 1940s and '50s is divided roughly along divisional lines.

At Whitford, where the double-track Philadelphia & Thorndale extension of the Trenton Cutoff crossed over the four-track Main Line at a shallow angle, hopper cars rumble overhead on the massive truss bridge while the Chicago-New York *Admiral* roars toward its station stop at Paoli behind a GG1. Photo by David G. Knox.

Philadelphia Terminal and Philadelphia Division

The Philadelphia-Harrisburg portion of the Main Line in the 1940s and '50s followed the old Philadelphia & Columbia as far as Lancaster, though a century of improvements left little of its original alignment intact. At Lancaster the Main Line picked up the path of the Harrisburg, Portsmouth, Mountjoy & Lancaster. The 103-mile line through hilly southeastern Pennsylvania did not follow any major waterways. So while line relocations had straightened out curves, they could not eliminate the grades: up out of the Schuylkill valley, down into the big valley west of Paoli and out again, up and down across country, and down into the Susquehanna valley.

Before track reductions in the late 1950s and '60s, four tracks were in use to Harrisburg, except for two double-track segments: the Conestoga Creek bridge just east of Lancaster, and the largely passenger-only Lancaster-Royalton portion. PRR practice was to number tracks consecutively from the south. In four-track territory, normal track assignments were outside tracks 1 and 4 for passenger trains, inside 2 and 3 for freight. Top allowable speeds were 75 mph for passenger trains (70 east of Paoli) and 50 for freight.

Philadelphia stations

While an 1850 relocation of the east terminus of the Philadelphia & Columbia to West Philadelphia was an improvement over the original site up the Schuylkill River at Belmont, it was still inconveniently located across the river from the center of the city. By the late 1870s PRR had determined to extend its track from the West Philly station site at 32nd and Market streets to the northwest corner of Broad and Market. Originally the geographic and always the figurative center of the city, the intersection was the site of Philadelphia's new city hall. Broad Street Station's Victorian Gothic head house and twin four-track sheds opened in 1881. By 1893 a 591-foot-long,

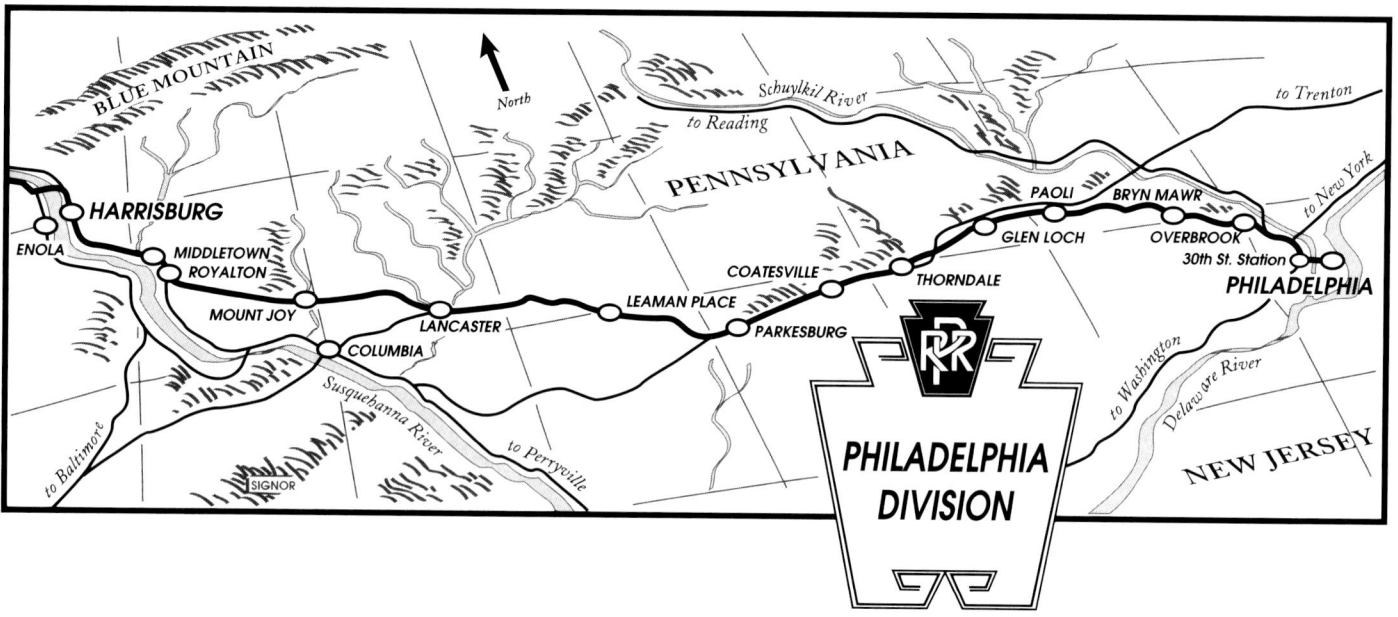

100-foot-high, 306-foot-wide shed covered 16 tracks, and the head house, having grown to a city block in width and 10 stories in height, was being readied to receive the road's general and executive offices.

PRR proudly dubbed Broad Street "America's Grandest Railway Terminal," but it was not without problems. Its stub-end configuration and location off the New York-Washington and New York-Pittsburgh routes made it operationally inconvenient. The company retained the West Philadelphia station and developed North Philadelphia station as the city's station for time-sensitive east-west trains. Moreover, the massive "Chinese Wall" that carried tracks above street level from the Schuylkill to Broad Street was the object of increasing public scorn. A fire in 1923 destroyed the big shed, which was replaced by umbrella sheds; another blaze occurred in 1943, but by then "Old Broad's" successors were already in place, and the station closed nine years later.

Two stations assumed Broad Street's functions. Broad Street Suburban Station was an underground terminal topped by an office building just to the north of Broad Street Station proper. All suburban trains (except a handful of steam-powered ones) moved to the new facility in 1930, as did PRR's headquarters offices. Trains climbed a steep grade up to the Chinese Wall tracks, which they joined to cross the Schuylkill on a single new bridge.

Across the river, Pennsy replaced the 32nd and Market station with a colossal new one at 30th Street. The new station had an upper level (opened in 1930) for trains from Suburban and Broad,

12

and a lower level (1933), originally planned to handle all PRR intercity trains (including the east-west fleet, which would turn on a loop south of the station) as well as those of the Reading and Baltimore & Ohio. This "union station" scheme never came to pass, and the loop track was never built, leaving Pennsy initially with too large a station for Depression-era traffic. Though 30th Street became the station for New York-Washington trains, Broad Street's location allowed it to hang on for Philadelphia-New York "Clockers" and Philadelphia-Harrisburg Main Line trains.

Branches and connections

In Philadelphia, the Main Line connected with the PRR's important lines to New York and Washington at Zoo Junction, and with the Schuylkill Branch to Reading and other anthracite country points at 52nd Street. Minor lines diverged at Frazer, Downingtown, Pomeroy, Lancaster, and Conewago. Other Pennsy lines intersecting the Main Line were more in the nature of alternative trunk-line freight routes than lines meant to tap new territory. The Trenton Cutoff, which left the New York Division just west of its namesake New Jersey city, connected at Glen Loch, beyond which an extension of the Cutoff, the Philadelphia & Thorndale Branch, paralleled the Main Line to Thorndale, where it finally joined. To the west, the Atglen & Susquehanna Branch offered freights a low-gradient parallel to the Main Line: it diverged at Parkesburg, went through Columbia, crossed the Susquehanna River, and joined the Northern Central from Baltimore at Wago Junction, 20 miles downriver from Enola Yard. The Columbia Branch followed the west end of the old Philadelphia & Columbia from Lancaster to the Susquehanna, whose east bank it then followed to Royalton. Although it didn't connect with the Main Line itself, the Columbia & Port Deposit Branch left the Maryland Division's Philadelphia-Washington line at Perryville, Maryland, then hugged the Susquehanna to Columbia, where it fed freights for Harrisburg and Enola to the A&S and Columbia branches.

The Philadelphia Division connected with Reading Company branch lines at Downingtown, Coatesville, Lancaster, Landisville, and Middletown, and with the Reading's east-west main line at Harrisburg. Also, a track at Zoo connected with Reading's portion of the Jersey City-Washington "Royal Blue Line." At Leaman Place, PRR connected with the Strasburg Rail Road, the ancient (1832) short line that was reborn in 1959 as one of the first steam tourist roads.

Electrification

The Pennsylvania's greatest 20th century project, the electrification of its eastern lines, began with the Philadelphia-Paoli section of the Main Line. By 1913, booming traffic on PRR's suburban lines caused severe congestion at Broad Street Station — 500 trains used the station daily, each requiring multiple moves because of the need to turn and service steam engines. PRR decided to electrify its two busiest lines, to Paoli and Chestnut Hill, and equip them with multiple-unit cars. With an eye toward electrifying part of its long-haul network, perhaps all the way to Pittsburgh, the railroad forsook the 600-volt DC third-rail system in use at its New York terminal for an 11,000-volt AC overhead catenary installation of the type that had recently proved itself on the New Haven Railroad. After electric operation began in September 1915, Main Line commuters enjoyed cleaner, faster service aboard MP54 MU cars, and Broad Street's capacity crunch was eased.

PRR extended catenary to New York and Washington and various branches throughout the 1920s and early '30s. The electrification was no longer just for suburban trains, but for all classes of traffic, and Pennsy developed several types of electric locomotives. In 1937 and 1938 wires went up over the remainder of the Main Line to Harrisburg, as well as over its associated freight lines. The work was completed just in time: World War II flooded the east end of the PRR with traffic, and the efficiencies of electrified operations were invaluable in keeping it moving.

The 1950s brought uncertainty to the electrified network, as the railroad studied options ranging from scrapping the line-haul portions of it in favor of diesels to extending electrification to Pittsburgh. The decade ended with the system intact, new generations of MU cars and freight locomotives on the horizon, and the great GG1 fleet handling a diminishing number of east-west passenger trains.

Traffic and operations

Philadelphia-Paoli traffic was dominated by "Paoli Local" MU trains serving the posh suburbs that took their collective name from the Main Line itself. These trains operated out of Suburban Station and were concentrated at rush hours. At Paoli, the location of PRR's system MU shop on the north side of the tracks, a duckunder track allowed originating eastbound trains to enter the Main Line without crossing any tracks. In 1941, there were 80 suburban trains each weekday (all figures are totals of east- and westbound schedules); by 1956, the total had grown to about 110. Some turned halfway out at Bryn Mawr and a handful extended west to Parkesburg. Longer-haul trains consisted of everything from a Philadelphia-Lancaster local to New York/Philadelphia-Harrisburg/Pittsburgh day trains to PRR's "Blue Ribbon Fleet" of overnighters to the Midwest. This traffic accounted for nearly 60 trains a day on the eve of World War II, but just under 50 by 1956. The premier New York trains entered the Main Line via the New York & Pittsburgh Subway, a line under the complex trackwork at Zoo built especially for them; most stopped only at Paoli and Lancaster, covering the division in about 2 hours 10 minutes.

Freights from the New York Division and the Philadelphia waterfront also entered at Zoo, which was just east of the 52nd Street hump yard. Trains from east of Trenton with no business in Philadelphia would bypass the city via the Trenton Cutoff. Virtually all freight then left the Main Line at Parkesburg (or Lancaster) to follow the Susquehanna to Harrisburg or Enola. Grades dictated helpers in both directions: heavy westbounds got them from Zoo to Paoli and from Thorndale to Parkesburg; big eastbounds were assisted from Thorndale to Paoli.

Brand-new GG1 4845 stands at Broad Street Station in 1935. Three Philadelphia landmarks rise behind the shiny G: City Hall tower, the dominant feature of the city's skyline for more than 80 years; the Philadelphia Savings Fund Society building, an early masterpiece of modern architecture; and the craggy Broad Street head building, home for more than three decades to Pennsy's headquarters, which looked down on the station's bumping posts — milepost 0 on the Main Line to the west. PRR photo.

The Suburban Station Building rises (left-center) in Art Deco modernity beside the umbrella trainsheds of hulking, Victorian Gothic Broad Street Station (bottom). The two stations coexisted for 22 years before "Old Broad's" closure in 1952. At the far end of Benjamin Franklin Parkway stands the Philadelphia Museum of Art (top), above which is visible the stone-arch bridge carrying PRR's New York Division across the Schuylkill River. PRR photo.

Taken before the construction of the Pennsylvania Boulevard bridge (later renamed John F. Kennedy Boulevard) and the Schuylkill Expressway, this view shows the proximity of 30th Street Station to the west bank of the Schuylkill River. In the foreground, near the bridge over Baltimore & Ohio's "Royal Blue Line" tracks, a wire crew tends to the catenary over the tracks leading from Suburban Station. Beyond the station are a PRR office building, the steam plant for the station complex (far right), and the West Philadelphia Elevated, the "High Line," a bypass for freight trains. Photo by J. B. Fuller, May 1, 1952.

E6s 4-4-2 645 brings a train into 30th Street's upper level on a gray day. The train was one of the last steam runs out of Broad Street Station, and 645 was among the last of the 83 E6s Atlantics (built from 1912 to 1914) in service. At right, a GG1 stands on storage tracks that served Broad Street. Photo by Wayne P. Ellis, Rail Photo Service, 1952.

A New York-bound "Clocker" from Broad Street pauses at 30th Street. With the closure of Broad Street, such trains moved to the lower level of 30th Street, beneath the main mass of the building. PRR photo.

A two-car train of new Budd-built Pioneer III MU cars skirts the maze of tracks at Zoo on its way in from Paoli. Zoo tower is visible in the background about a third of the way in from the right side of the picture; farther to the right can be seen part of Centennial Hall, built for the world's fair in 1876. Photo by Aaron G. Fryer, 1958.

At Overbrook, first of the 17 stations serving the leafy "Main Line" suburbs and a popular spot to watch trains, five MP54s on a rush-hour Paoli Local schedule grind west on a dreary, snowy afternoon. The position-light signal at right indicates "clear" for the next eastbound movement on track 1. Photo by Aaron G. Fryer, February 1, 1957.

A boxcab P5a brings a mixed freight east through Overbrook in the aftermath of a February 1958 storm whose exceptionally fine snowflakes crippled the GG1 fleet by fouling the locomotives' electrical systems. The P5s were able to carry on because their air intakes were mounted higher above the rail (and above the level at which the tiny snow particles formed). Photo by Aaron G. Fryer.

GG1 4899 whisks Harrisburg-Philadelphia train 604 past the interlocking tower (visible above the locomotive) and 1858 station building (above the B60 baggage car) at Overbrook. Photo by Aaron G. Fryer, March 1957.

Bound for Greenwich Yard in South Philadelphia, a GG1 swings through Overbrook with an eastbound merchandise train. Built for passenger service between 1934 and 1943, the 139 Gs proved to be capable freight haulers. Photo by Aaron G. Fryer, March 19, 1956.

A train of MP54s, workhorses of PRR's electrified suburban lines, comes into Merion from Paoli in the mid-1940s. Passengers wait to board in front of the ticket office and waiting room; across the tracks on the westbound side, a similar but larger building (just out of view) houses the Merion Station post office. Photo by J. A. McLellan.

Slogging through a storm that dumped 15 to 35 inches of snow on parts of Pennsylvania, New Jersey, and New York, the *Broadway Limited,* leader of PRR's great east-west fleet, rolls through Merion toward Philadelphia and New York. Photo by Richard S. Short, March 20, 1958.

Framed by platform canopy and passengers, MP54s occupy both outside tracks at Wayne in a 1950s scene that changed little from 1915 to 1975. Pennsy had more than 400 of the owl-faced MU cars, many of them rebuilt from steam-hauled coaches. Photo by Elizabeth Hibbs.

Two Budd Pioneer III cars (PRR class MP85) depart Paoli on a test run. In 1958, as the MP54 fleet increasingly felt — and showed — its age, Pennsy bought six prototype stainless-steel MU cars. They were the basis for the many Silverliners and Jersey Arrows that replaced the MP54s in the late 1970s. Photo by Pier Clifford, June 18, 1958.

At Glen Loch, 5.4 miles beyond the end of suburban territory at Paoli, boxcab P5a 4710 works hard to pull a westbound freight up onto track 3 from the Trenton Cutoff. The short connector from the cutoff ducks under the Main Line's two westbound tracks in a classic PRR flying junction. Photo by Charles A. Elston.

The toughest grades on the Main Line east of the Alleghenies were between Philadelphia and Harrisburg. L1s 2-8-2 No. 714 helps a P5a on an eastbound freight at Downingtown; added to the train at Thorndale, 2.7 miles to the west, the steamer will help the train as far as Paoli. Photo by C. A. Brown, August 17, 1946.

Pusher engineer and rear-end crewman confer at Thorndale before FF2 No. 6 gives a boost to freight NY-8, eastbound via the Trenton Cutoff. Built in the 1920s for Great Northern's Cascade Tunnel line, No. 6 was one of eight motors GN sold to Pennsy after pulling the plug on its electrified district in 1956. PRR numbered them 1 to 7 (with the eighth used for parts) and used the powerful but slow boxcabs mostly as helpers between Philadelphia and Harrisburg. Photos by Don Wood, February 1, 1958.

Just east of Thorndale, P5a 4755 is about to duck under the west end of the Trenton Cutoff as it heads a freight east on the Main Line's track 2. Catenary poles for the two westbound tracks are visible at left above the embankment at this flying junction. Conceived in the early 1930s, the P5a failed as a passenger hauler but became PRR's principal freight motor until the early '60s. Photo by Bert Pennypacker.

A GG1 with Williamsport-Philadelphia train 526, the *Susquehannock,* slams past a modified P5a at Thorndale. After a 1934 accident killed the crew of a boxcab P5a, the design for subsequent units was modified to a streamlined steeple-cab configuration. Photo by Bert Pennypacker.

With low-grade freight lines feeding the Main Line at Thorndale to the east and Parkesburg to the west, Coatesville saw concentrated freight traffic. Here a single modified P5a whines up the 0.6 percent westbound grade that necessitated pushers on many trains out of Thorndale. Photo by Bert Pennypacker.

The old, the transitional, and the new team up on a westbound at Coatesville. Representing PRR's early designs are boxcab and modified P5a motors. The third and fourth units are General Electric AC-motored E2b Nos. 4944 and 4942, two of a handful of straight-AC and AC-DC cab units Pennsy acquired in the early 1950s as a prelude to replacing the P5a fleet. The hood unit is E44 No. 4411, one of 66 AC-DC rectifier units whose arrival in the early '60s spelled the end for the P5a and the experimentals. The two lead units were added to the train when the road engines developed problems. Photo by Frank Tatnall, November 23, 1961.

GG1s meet at Royalton, where the Port Road freight line from Perryville, Maryland, joins the Main Line. Seen from the fireman's seat of the G on train 72, the *Juniata,* 4863 approaches with train 75, the *Duquesne.* No. 4863's raised forward pantograph suggests trouble with the trailing one, which PRR preferred to use. Photo by David G. Knox.

One of the best-remembered rituals of PRR operations was the engine change at Harrisburg. Here, GG1 4858 has brought train 33, the *St. Louisan,* in from New York and is moving into the clear, to be replaced by a set of EMD E7s. The ornate building behind the diesels is the Reading Company's station. Photo by Bert Pennypacker, June 8, 1952.

At the east end of Harrisburg station, 4884 backs down to the eastbound *Pennsylvania Limited.* In the distance are the train's diesels with some head-end cars for Harrisburg, and an SW1 station switcher. Photo by J. E. Bradley, November 1965.

Beyond Harrisburg's iron-and-wood trainshed, railroad men exchange small talk at the head end of train 77, the *Trail Blazer.* An A-B-A set of Baldwin DR6-4-20 "Sharknose" passenger diesels will forward the train to Chicago. PRR's 18 A units and 9 B units of 1948 were the only passenger Sharknoses built. Photo by Al Rung.

38

A view down from the concourse of Harrisburg station reveals platform sweepers, passengers, baggage carts, and lots of train activity, including a B1 six-wheel electric switcher cutting a coach off a train. Photo by Linn H. Westcott, April 1948.

Two symbols of the standard era of railroading — a K4s Pacific and a heavyweight Pullman sleeper — stand at Harrisburg. On this day, *Rathbone* was serving as the set-out sleeper for train 35, the *Pittsburgh Night Express,* which paused in Harrisburg at 1 a.m. on its run from Broad Street. Photo by Al Rung, 1939.

On a cold night, two K4s locomotives stand ready to take their trains west. Most of PRR's "Blue Ribbon Fleet" called at Harrisburg in darkness, evening westbound and morning eastbound. Photo by Al Rung.

No. 6110, one of two prototype T1 duplex-drive 4-4-4-4 passenger engines built in 1942, stands at Harrisburg two days after the surrender of Japan ended World War II. Fifty production models came in the 12 months following the war. Photo by Theo. A. Gay, August 16, 1945.

K4s Pacifics 5334 and 3820 hammer out of Harrisburg with a 13-car train, probably the *St. Louisan.* Soon they will leave behind the state capital's complex trackwork and wire-bound skies, curve onto the Rockville Bridge across the Susquehanna River, and enter the wide open spaces of the Middle Division. Photo by J. W. Maxwell, April 1942.

M1a 4-8-2 6743, not yet fitted with the drop-coupler pilot that was typical of the class in the postwar years, heels to the sharp curve just east of Lewistown with an eastbound freight. Photo by John P. Ahrens, October 1947.

MIDDLE DIVISION

While the Middle Division of the 1940s and early '50s actually began 7 miles west of Harrisburg at Marysville, in spirit it started at the state capital, where the Pennsylvania began its push west a century before, and where electric motive power yielded to steam and diesel. The rambling old wood-and-metal trainshed at Harrisburg served as something of a transition between PRR's bustling eastern lines and the bucolic heartland of the Keystone State. And the great stone-arch Rockville Bridge of 1902 over the wide Susquehanna, joining steep mountainsides at either end, symbolized the geographic challenges that lay to the west, even though the Middle Division's own profile wasn't particularly rugged. With minor realignments, it followed J. Edgar Thomson's river-valley path to the base of the Alleghenies; its steepest grade was less than 0.5 percent, encountered on the last 30 miles before Altoona.

The 131-mile line from Harrisburg to Altoona was mostly four tracks wide. An exception to Pennsy's customary track assignments of outside passenger and inside freight was between Marysville (where the freight tracks from Enola Yard joined the Main Line) and Duncannon. This 6-mile stretch was signaled as two parallel double-track railroads, with tracks 1 and 2 for trains (mostly passenger) that crossed the Rockville Bridge and 3 and 4 for freights running in and out of Enola. The twisting 8 miles between the Spruce Creek tunnels and Tyrone had only three tracks, while Tyrone-Altoona boasted five. In 1955 track 3 was removed between Newport and Mifflin. Top speeds were 70 mph for passenger trains, 50 for freight. Track pans for steam engines to scoop water on the fly were located at Bailey, Hawstone, Mapleton, and Bellwood.

Enola Yard

Situated across the Susquehanna from Harrisburg, Enola Yard was assigned to the Philadelphia Division, but it catered to trains of the Maryland, Middle, and Susquehanna divisions as well. It was another of the Pennsy's ambitious turn-of-the-century improvement projects, and it became the largest freight yard in the world. Enola was really four yards: eastbound receiving and hump yards, and westbound receiving and hump. In 1953 Enola's 192 tracks had a capacity of 12,888 cars, just a few more than the number of cars that passed through in a given day. The enginehouse, which was a home base for 248 diesels, 90 electrics, and 70 steamers, serviced about 160 road, switcher, and shop locomotives each day. Some 4,000 employees reported for work in each 24-hour period. In addition to repairing 50 to 80 bad-order cars, Enola rebuilt 13 open-top cars each day. Most Middle Division freights began or ended their runs at Enola, though a few operated via Harrisburg.

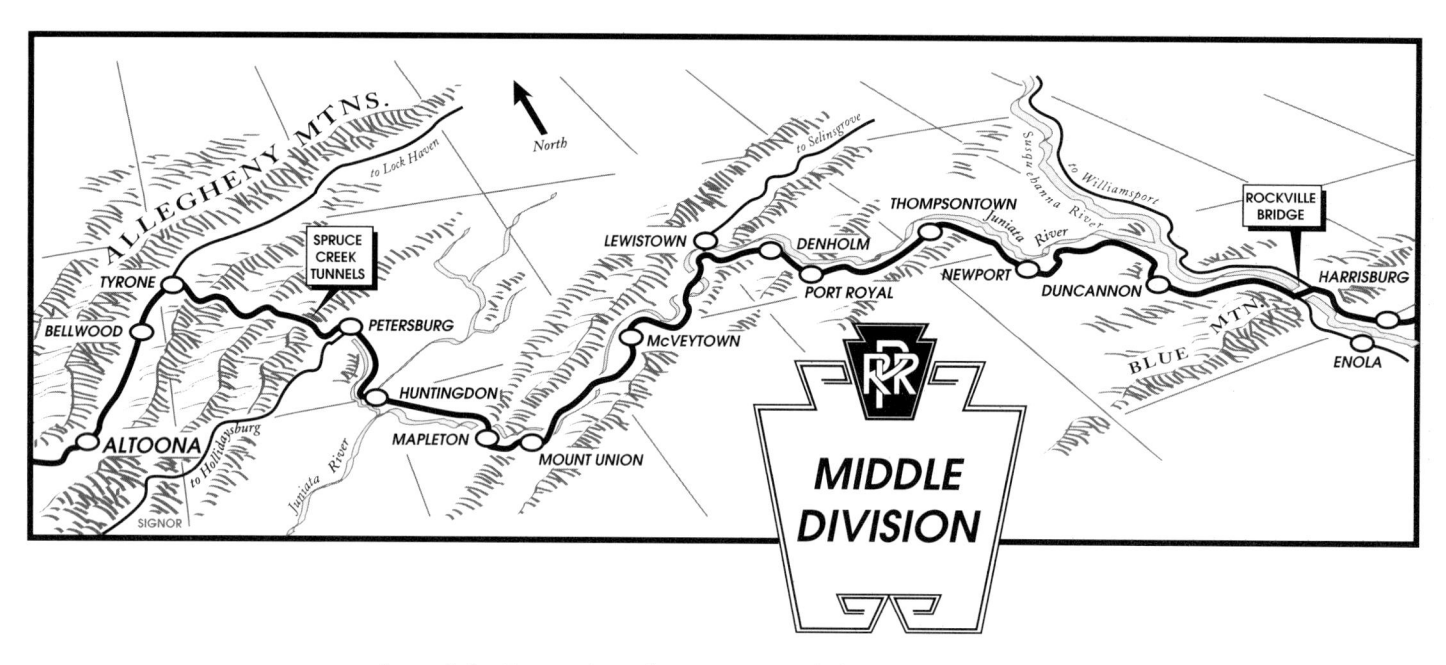

Branches and connections

A passenger out of Harrisburg would note the tracks of the Susquehanna Division to upstate Pennsylvania and New York heading straight up the east bank of the river as his train turned left to cross the Rockville Bridge. On the far side, a flying junction merged the lines from Enola (originally the Northern Central) with the Main Line. At Lewistown, the line from Selinsgrove Junction (just below Sunbury on the Susquehanna Division) joined, together with a short branch north to Milroy. The Hollidaysburg & Petersburg Secondary diverged from the Main Line at Petersburg, providing freights with an alternate route to the foot of the Alleghenies. At Tyrone the Bald Eagle Branch came in from Lock Haven on the Susquehanna Division.

The PRR connected with only two other railroads on the Middle Division, the 3-foot gauge East Broad Top at Mount Union, and the 64-mile Huntingdon & Broad Top Mountain at Huntingdon. EBT interchanged cars with the Pennsy by swapping their standard gauge trucks for narrow gauge ones. Both roads fell victim to the decline of the coal industry and closed in the mid-1950s, though a part of the EBT was reborn as a tourist line.

Traffic and operations

PRR's Blue Ribbon Fleet of passenger trains came into its own on the Middle Division. The 1941 timetable shows 55 daily passenger trains, 41 with names. Fifteen years later, elimination of local schedules and combination of long-haul trains cut the total to 32, all but one named. As 1960 dawned, only 21 passenger trains traversed the division each day. The top trains made the trip in 2½ hours, with no intermediate stops. The show was chiefly nocturnal, with trains scheduled to depart eastern cities in the late afternoon or evening and arrive in the morning.

Altoona

If the brains of the PRR were in Philadelphia, its brawn was in Altoona. The railroad built yards and shops there when it established an operating base for its assault on the Allegheny Mountains. From an eight-stall roundhouse and a single shop building, the Altoona facilities grew into the largest group of railroad shops in the world. By the time production ended in 1946, Altoona had built 6,873 locomotives. In that year, Altoona Works — the collective name for Altoona Machine Shop, Altoona Car Shops, Juniata Shops, and South Altoona Foundries — sprawled over 218 acres near the center of the city. The 125 shop buildings alone covered 65 acres. Some 12,000 people worked there, 15 percent of the city's total population. In addition to its construction and repair functions, Altoona was home to PRR's comprehensive test department. It evaluated virtually everything used on the railroad, from dining-car supplies to locomotives; the latter were put through their paces on a unique stationary test plant installed in 1905. In East Altoona, a massive roundhouse and a classification yard catered to the operational needs of the Main Line. The 1950s were not kind to Altoona — the end of steam saw massive cutbacks in facilities and employment, and a new system carshop was opened in nearby Hollidaysburg.

With the icy Susquehanna River below, an L1s Mikado heads a local freight eastward across the Rockville Bridge. Photo by Wayne P. Ellis, Rail Photo Service, February 1954.

Two E8s lead the mixture of head-end, streamlined, and heavyweight cars making up the eastbound *Juniata* onto the Rockville Bridge. Photo by Philip R. Hastings, 1952.

As one M1 blasts toward Altoona (foreground), another brings a freight from Williamsport across the Susquehanna. Soon the distant train will pass over the westbound on its way into Enola Yard. Photo by Philip R. Hastings, 1952.

Smoke rockets skyward and drivers spin as M1b 6749 struggles to restart an eastbound train at the west end of the Rockville Bridge. Photo by Ralph W. Hull, November 12, 1955.

Steam, diesel, and electric locomotives mingle at the center of PRR's colossal Enola Yard. EMD F units head a train into the eastbound receiving yard; the westbound receiving tracks are visible beyond the engine terminal at the center of the picture. Photo by Philip R. Hastings.

L1s 714 retrieves a boxcar routed to the wrong track at Enola's westbound hump. It's a measure of PRR's size that its 574 World War I-era L1s "Lollipops" were only its second largest locomotive class. Photo by Philip R. Hastings.

At the west end of Enola Yard, three new GP9s meet a four-unit F7 set. The Geeps have just crossed the Rockville Bridge with a 78-car train off the Susquehanna Division; the Fs are on train PG-8, headed for the Middle Division. Photo by Don Wood, December 1955.

At Perdix, west of the convergence of the Rockville Bridge and Enola lines at Marysville, I1sa 2-10-0 4594 rolls empty hoppers toward Altoona. Trailing a new 16-wheel, all-welded tender longer than the engine itself, the old Decapod thunders by the overhead water cranes without stopping. Photo by Don Wood.

Just over three years after the photo on the opposite page, two Baldwin freight Sharknoses handle a similar train past the same spot — but the water facilities are gone. Photo by F. R. Kern, Jay Potter collection, January 1959.

In a marvelous view of men and machinery at work, M1b 6736 rolls tonnage west through Perdix with the engineer at the throttle, the fireman checking the coal supply, and the head-end brakeman in his doghouse. Photo by Don Wood, September 1956.

Two sets of Baldwin's distinctive DR-12-8-1500/2, or "Centipede," diesels meet 1½ miles east of Duncannon. Unreliable in passenger service, for which they were built in 1947, PRR's 12 two-unit Centipede sets spent most of their 15-year careers in freight and helper service. Photo by F. R. Kern, Jay Potter collection, January 1959.

General Motors' lightweight *Aerotrain* swings through Duncannon at the end of a year-long stint in New York–Pittsburgh service. Hidden behind the train is View tower, named for the broad Susquehanna valley vistas its operators enjoyed. Photo by Paul Carleton, June 29, 1957.

With a low trail of smoke suggesting it is making the 70 mph track speed, K4s 299 gallops up the Juniata River valley with the *Duquesne* west of Bailey. Photo by Donald Furler, July 20, 1941.

F units in A-B-B-A formation roll freight east through Port interlocking at Newport. Photo by Don Wood, May 1955.

In a beautiful Juniata valley setting worthy of a Grif Teller calendar painting, two brand-new E8s sail through Millerstown with the westbound *Manhattan Limited* for Chicago. Photo by Fred McLeod, July 1952.

The Main Line has just been reduced to three tracks between Newport and Mifflin, but the action is still heavy as three F units on an eastbound freight meet a westbound at Thompsontown. Photo by Don Wood, December 31, 1955.

At the massive coal wharf that spanned the widened Main Line at Denholm, M1 6921 gets under way with PG-5 after topping off coal and water supplies. Photo by Don Wood.

63

Again at Denholm, two shots from August 1956 show M1 6921 doubleheading behind 6717 on an ore drag for Pittsburgh. Photos by Don Wood.

Middle Division Monarch: The M1

Late in life, M1 6888, a 1926 Baldwin, rides the turntable at the East Altoona enginehouse. Photo by Don Wood, September 6, 1956.

The dual-service M1 4-8-2 Mountain was neither PRR's most numerous nor its most sophisticated locomotive class, but many regard it as the Pennsy's best steam power. Its greatest stage was the Middle Division.

Chesapeake & Ohio pioneered the 4-8-2 wheel arrangement in 1911 with two engines for mountain passenger service. Their low drivers (62 inches) and other features made them essentially Mikados with four-wheel leading trucks. A pair of Rock Island engines set the pattern for most subsequent 4-8-2s in 1913. They had 69-inch drivers and pulled heavy passenger trains on the plains of Kansas and Colorado. Despite its passenger inspiration, the 4-8-2 developed into a dual-service wheel arrangement. A total of 2201 Mountains were built for North American service; New York Central had the most, 600.

Searching for an engine that could handle both heavy passenger trains in the mountains and fast freights in level territory, PRR built a prototype 4-8-2 at Altoona in 1923. William Wallace Atterbury, PRR vice president-operations and later president, championed the project. No. 4700 was given class M1; since superheating had become a standard feature by this time, the "s" class suffix indicating that an engine was so equipped was omitted for the M1 and all subsequent classes.

In keeping with PRR's practice of standardization, the new locomotive's boiler, which carried a pressure of 250 pounds, was a near duplicate of that used on the I1s 2-10-0. Many other components matched those on other classes, as well. Originally designed to have 80-inch drivers like the K4s Pacific, the M1 received 72-inch wheels, a change that would greatly enhance its usefulness as a freight engine. The prototype had a small passenger tender and was hand-fired.

After testing, the first M1 was followed by 200 production models with slight variations, most notably larger tenders, stokers, and greater heating surface. Though built to passenger specifications, with bar pilots, chime whistles, and fancy striping, the new engines found their niche in freight service, where the market was placing increasing importance on speed. PRR at the time had no other engines to equal the Mountains' ability to haul tonnage fast.

Compared with the typically spare Pennsy engine, the 100 M1a locomotives were laden with special features, including huge 22,090-gallon tenders that the earlier M1 engines soon received as well. At 390,000 pounds, the M1a locomotives were a bit heavier than their older sisters, but possessed the same 64,550-pound tractive force. All but 10 were for freight service. A reboilering program begun in 1944 boosted tractive force to 69,700 pounds and meant reclassification to M1b for 40 of the class.

The construction history of PRR's Mountains is a simple one:

M1
6699	Altoona, 1923
6800–6974	Baldwin, 1926
6975–6999	Lima, 1926

M1a
6700–6749	Baldwin, 1930
6750–6774	Altoona, 1930
6775–6799	Lima, 1930

Notes: 6699 renumbered from 4700 in 1933. Between 1944 and 1953, 40 M1a engines changed to M1b.

The electrification of PRR's eastern lines in the 1930s meant that there were plenty of Pacifics to go around, even at two to a train, further emphasizing the M1's role as a freight engine. The Mountains were at their best on freights in relatively flat country; Pennsy assigned most of them to divisions west of Pittsburgh and to the Middle Division, where they made their last stand until just before the end of PRR steam in November 1957.

With a healthy count of head-end cars behind its two E8s, the *St. Louisan* heels to the curve at the west approach to Denholm. As one of the few members of the east-west fleet to traverse the Middle Division by daylight, train 32 was a popular photo subject. Photo by Wayne P. Ellis, Rail Photo Service.

Two views just east of Lewistown: T1 5548 blackens the sky — and its long mail-and-express train — as it roars west up track 4. M1a No. 6889, clean, still mated with a passenger tender, and displaying a partially modified front end — the headlight is new, but in the original location; the pilot is new, but with old-style marker lights — pulls coal empties westbound. Both photos by John P. Ahrens, October 4, 1947.

67

Two E8s bring a westbound mail-and-express train past an empty platform at Lewistown. When PRR's 74 E8s (all A units) joined its 60 E7As and Bs from 1950 through 1952, steam and most minority diesel makes were finished on all but the lowliest passenger runs. Photo by Don Wood, June 1956.

Like the T1 duplex steamers, the Baldwin Centipede diesels were soon bumped from top passenger assignments. Here a set passes Lewis tower just west of Lewistown with a westbound mail-and-express train. Photo by Clarence Weaver, William D. Volkmer collection.

M1 6979 passes over the Mapleton track pans on its way west with hotshot PG-5. These pans and those at Hawstone, 33 miles east, lasted nearly to the end of steam in 1957. Photo by Don Wood, September 22, 1956.

Its blower lifting smoke skyward, T1 5544 on an eastbound limited waits impatiently for baggagemen to complete their work at Huntingdon. Photo by Kenneth E. Pearson.

Under PRR's idiosyncratic numbering system, the 425-member K4s fleet was scattered between road numbers 8 and 8378. Engine 12, the second-lowest-numbered of the clan, wheels an eastbound troop train through Huntingdon. Compare its modified front end with the more classic appearance of the 5433 on page 40. Photo by William P. Price, October 7, 1946.

In a rearward view from atop a boxcar in a westbound freight, Spruce tower is nestled between the Little Juniata River and the Main Line just west of the Spruce Creek tunnels. Photo by Fred McLeod, July 10, 1938.

Toward the west end of the Middle Division, the Main Line crossed and recrossed the Little Juniata River. With a wave from the fireman, E8s lead the *St. Louisan* eastward over one of the many substantial stone-arch bridges east of Tyrone. Photo by Bob Lorenz, August 5, 1958.

Just a month before the end of steam on the PRR, Alco FAs swing through Tyrone with a westbound freight. Pennsy bought yard, road freight, and road passenger diesels from all major builders of the era; the FAs arrived on the property from 1948 to 1951. Photo by Ken Douglas, October 13, 1957.

Triple meet at Tyrone: Seen from the cabin car of westbound "TrucTrain" TT-1, Sharknoses on a train of perishables overtake coal hoppers trundling east. Photo by Don Wood, February 6, 1960.

Altoona! The Pennsylvania's central position — physically, economically, socially — in the city it founded at the base of the Alleghenies is apparent in this view. Stretching east from the shed of the passenger depot (center of photo) are some 5 miles of locomotive and car shops, engine houses, and freight yards. PRR photo.

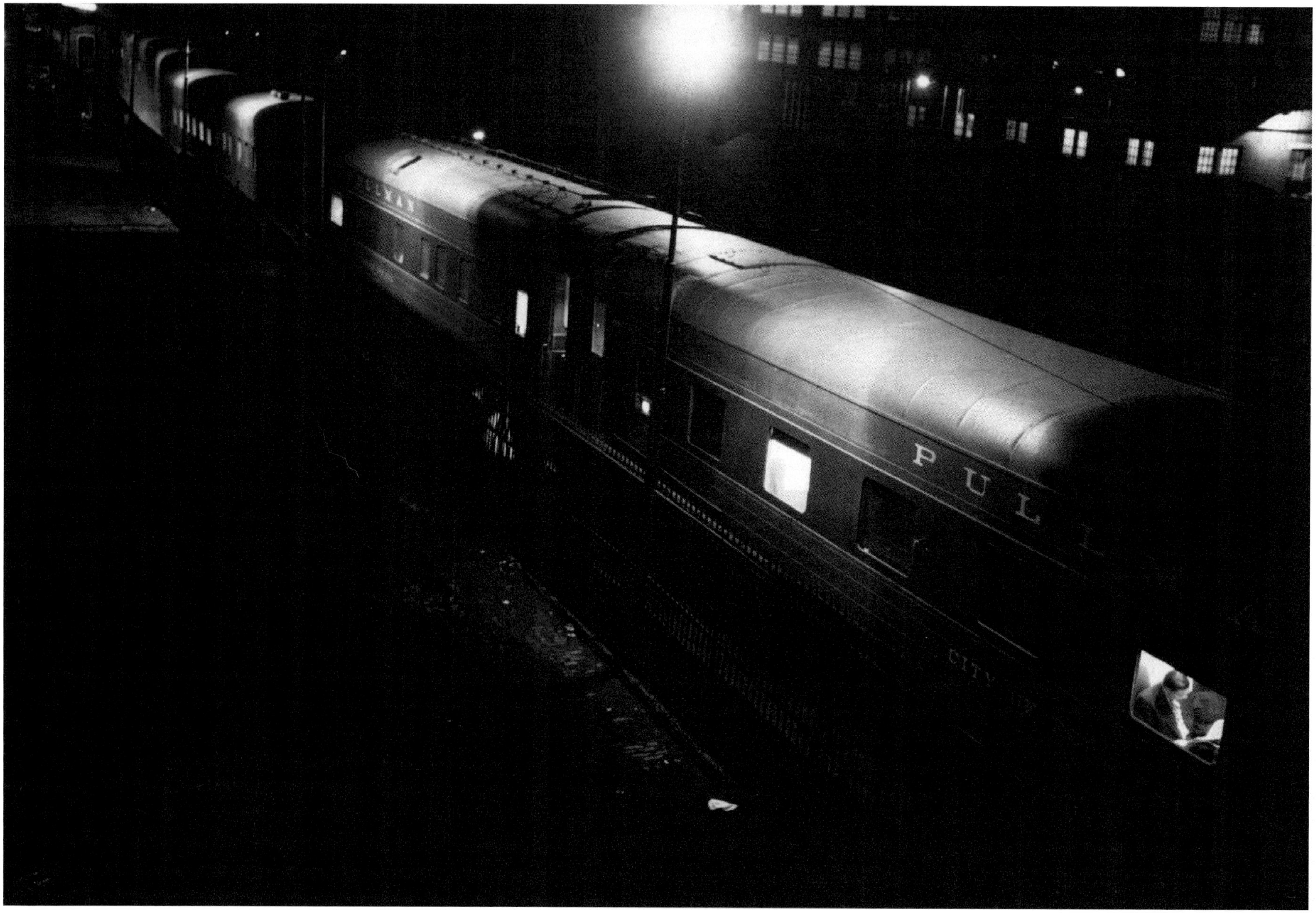
PUL

At night, Altoona saw a parade of trains in the Blue Ribbon Fleet. At 11:07, T1 5532 on the westbound *Cincinnati Limited* gets a going-over, the inspector's tour marked by the fiery trail of his torch. At 11:24 (opposite page), a *Broadway Limited* passenger reads the newspaper in his roomette during 29's brief stop. Two and a half hours later, a small group awaits the arrival of the eastbound *Manhattan Limited*. Three photos by Al Rung, April 1947.

With exhaust erupting volcano-like from its stack, J1 2-10-4 No. 6154 drags a mixed freight up the 1.8 percent grade of the PRR's most famous landmark: Horseshoe Curve. Photo by Fred McLeod.

Pittsburgh Division

In a landmark article in the April 1956 issue of *Trains* Magazine, then-editor David P. Morgan called the Altoona-Pittsburgh segment of the Pennsylvania's Main Line "the backbone, the core, the guts of the biggest railroad . . . in the Western Hemisphere." On the Pittsburgh Division, the hallmark of the PRR — exemplary engineering in the service of torrential traffic — was put to the test by rugged topography and a flood tide of through trains, locals, switch jobs, and light-engine moves. Pennsy's dramatic crossing of the Alleghenies just west of Altoona — highlighted by the famous Horseshoe Curve — and the sawtooth profile of the western half of the division were the price the railroad had to pay for access to the legions of coal mines between the mountains, steel plants around Pittsburgh, and traffic-heavy trunk lines of the Midwest.

PRR had four main tracks in use from Altoona to the west side of Johnstown and a fifth between Gallitzin and Cresson. From Johnstown to Conpitt Junction, tracks 1, 2, and 3 were separated by the Conemaugh River from tracks 5 and 6 (known as the Sang Hollow Extension), though all five tracks functioned as the Main Line. Beyond Conpitt, four tracks did the job as far as the Pittsburgh terminal area. Track assignments varied across the division's 114 miles: up the east slope of the Alleghenies the designations for tracks 1 to 4 were freight-passenger-freight-passenger, while outside freight/inside passenger prevailed beyond. Maximum speeds were 70 mph for passenger and 50 for freight, though curves and grades cut these figures nearly in half in many places. Water was available from track pans at Wilmore, Sang Hollow, Saxmans (Latrobe), and Homewood.

Horseshoe Curve and the East Slope

The Pennsy's climb out of Altoona is among the most celebrated stretches of railroad in the world, thanks chiefly to a dramatic feature about halfway up the hill: Horseshoe Curve. While laying out the PRR from Harrisburg, J. Edgar Thomson had maintained a relatively flat approach to the mountains. But between Altoona and the summit at Gallitzin, he was faced with lifting the railroad 1,000 feet in 12 miles. The path he chose took the line southwest out to Burgoon Run, which it followed west at a 1.75 percent grade until it encountered a sheer wall of rock, Kittanning Point — on either side of which were narrow ravines. The solution was to double the railroad back on itself in a great semicircle. By curving across the two ravines on fills and shaving off part of the rock face, the railroad was able to turn eastward. Beyond Horseshoe Curve, the grade stiffened to 1.86 percent as the rails turned south, then west again, high above Sugar Run. Four major curves later, the line entered the summit tunnel at Gallitzin.

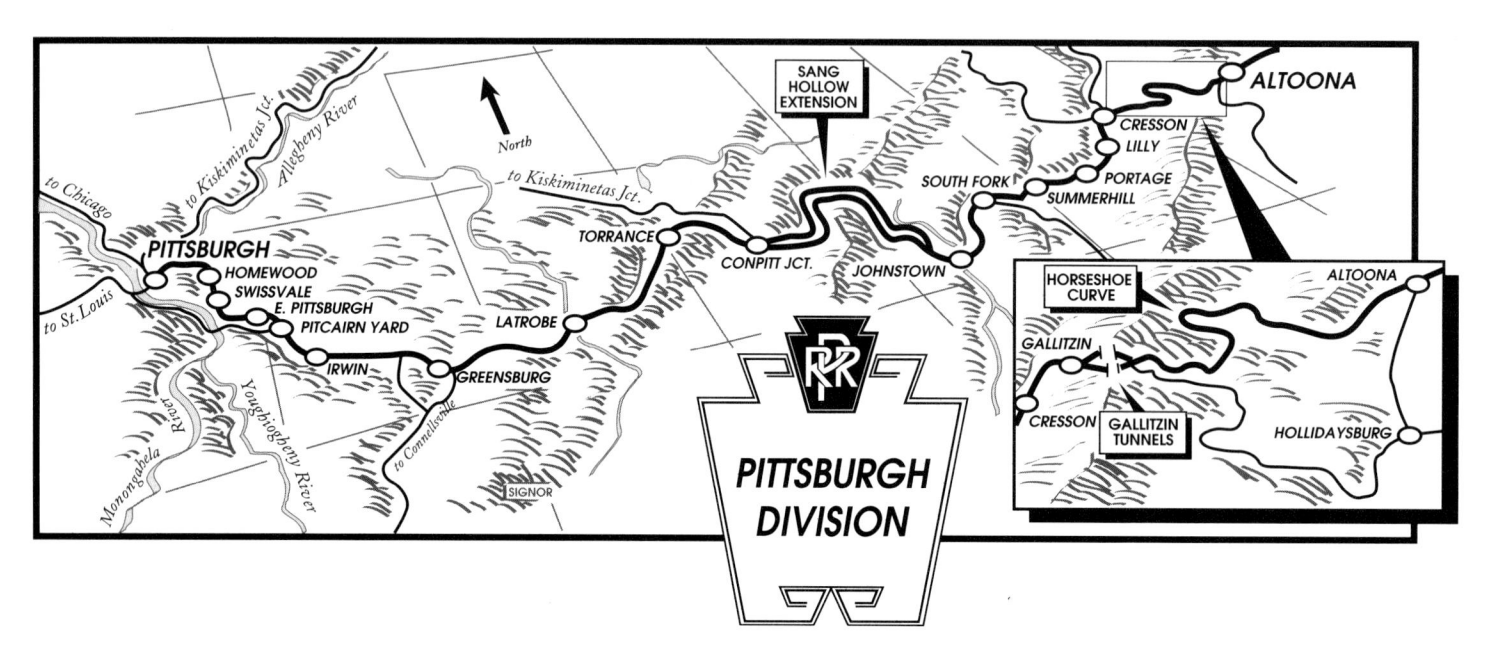

Surrounded on three sides by mountains, and with a long vista to the east, Horseshoe Curve was early recognized as a natural amphitheater for train-watching. Steam engines could be heard fighting up the grade long before they reached the Curve, and visitors to the small park established at its center in 1879 delighted in being nearly surrounded by long trains. By the 1940s, the principal challenge of the Pittsburgh Division as a whole — dense traffic on a mountain railroad — was best observed at the Curve, where a train was nearly always visible on the four-track right-of-way.

Traffic and operations

Pittsburgh Division passenger traffic during the 1940s and '50s mirrored that of the Middle Division, with the addition of commuter trains on the west end. Commuter trains ran in and out of Pittsburgh as far east as Derry to the tune of 40 each weekday in 1941 and half that 15 years later. Premier trains making no passenger stops took 2½ hours to go east or west between Altoona and Pittsburgh.

Virtually everything out of Altoona got a helper for the climb up the east slope to Gallitzin. On passenger trains, helpers were placed ahead of the road engine; freight helpers shoved from behind the cabin car. Heavy eastbound freights got a boost up the west slope, sometimes all the way from Pitcairn Yard, just east of Pittsburgh. With the advent of dynamic-brake-equipped diesels, helpers were routinely kept on freights through Gallitzin to assist with braking on downgrades.

Branches and connections

Many PRR lines left the Main Line between Altoona and Pittsburgh. Diverging southward at Alto tower, just west of the Altoona passenger station, part of the original (pre-Horseshoe Curve) Main Line survived as the Hollidaysburg & Petersburg Branch. At Duncansville, this line encountered the H&P Secondary from Petersburg to the east, and the New Portage Branch from Gallitzin to the west. The latter was laid on the grade of the state system's New Portage Railroad, abandoned in 1857 but reopened by the PRR in 1904. Together these lines formed an alternate route around Altoona and the Main Line's assault on the east slope; the bypass rejoined the Main Line just east of the Gallitzin tunnels. At Cresson, two branches funneled in coal traffic from a network of lines to the north and west. On a similar mission, the South Fork Branch twisted south, passing through the remains of the dam whose failure caused the Johnstown Flood in 1889. At Conpitt Junction, the Conemaugh Division main line followed its namesake river northwest to the Allegheny River, which then took it to Pittsburgh, providing a water-level alternative to the Pittsburgh Division's undulating profile. On either side of Greensburg, lines diverged, joined just south of Greensburg, and continued southward as the Southwest Secondary.

At Trafford, 17 miles east of Pittsburgh, the Turtle Creek Branch came in from Saltsburg on the Conemaugh main. Just west of Pitcairn Yard, the Port Perry Branch diverged, crossed the Monongahela River, and joined the Monongahela Branch, which served as a freight bypass around downtown Pittsburgh. In Pittsburgh itself, the Brilliant Branch linked the Main Line with the Allegheny Branch and the Conemaugh main to the north; this offered yet another route by which freights could avoid the congestion at Pennsylvania Station, where the Main Line split into the Fort Wayne and Panhandle main lines. Minor branches were at Lilly, Cassandra, Portage, Derry, Latrobe, Donohoe, Manor, and Shafton.

As on the eastern portions of the Main Line, the PRR encountered few railroads between Altoona and Pittsburgh: a Baltimore & Ohio branch and the shortline Conemaugh & Black Lick at Johnstown, the electric interurban Ligonier Valley at Latrobe, the Union Railroad at East Pittsburgh, and the B&O again at Pittsburgh.

Pittsburgh

As the hub of the Pennsylvania's 13-state system, Pittsburgh was to the PRR what Chicago was to the national railroad network as a whole: a source of both fabulous traffic and vexing terminal difficulties. As they reached the city in the 1850s and '60s, the PRR and its affiliated lines established separate stations near the confluence of the Allegheny and Monongahela rivers. Pennsy's original station of 1851 was succeeded three years later by the first of four "union stations" — although the PRR proper, the Fort Wayne, and the Panhandle did not share the same facility until after the Civil War. The second union station, like many other PRR properties in Pittsburgh, was a casualty of the fires stemming from the labor riots of 1877. All the major stations were located between the two rivers — about a mile east of the head of the Ohio River — near the Liberty Avenue and Grant Street site of the fourth and final depot.

By the late 1890s, growth of both the city and the railroad's traffic had made an intolerable situation of the ground-level trackage serving the third Pennsy depot. Work began in 1901 on track elevation and on a new 12-story Pennsylvania Station with an elegant rotunda and a trainshed measuring 258 feet wide by 556 feet long. The project was difficult, thanks to the proximity not only of Grant's Hill and the Panhandle's tunnel through it on the south, but of the Fort Wayne's bridge over the Allegheny on the north. The need to maintain train service in this confined area added further complications. After World War II, as part of a general plan to clean up downtown Pittsburgh, PRR poured $27 million into station improvements: low, glass-and-steel trainsheds to replace the barnlike, single-span original; a realigned approach to the Fort Wayne bridge; pedestrian underpasses from the waiting room to the tracks; and complete remodeling of the waiting room and gate concourse.

The postwar period saw improvements to Pennsy freight facilities as well. A new, four-block-long freight house arose just north of Pennsylvania Station, replacing old depots in the waterfront Point area. Twenty miles west on the north bank of the Ohio River, PRR expanded and modernized Conway Yard, making it the company's major Pittsburgh freight-classification yard when it was completed in 1956. Although Pitcairn — some 15 miles east of downtown and the main yard on the west end of the Pittsburgh Division — was still a major facility in the postwar period, it was downgraded after Conway's completion.

At aptly named Slope interlocking, a J1 storms uphill out of Altoona, attacking the grade railroaders called simply "the mountain." Photo by Linn H. Westcott, April 1948.

Semaphores have not quite given way entirely to position-light signals in this early postwar view of a T1 with a limited from the west rolling into Altoona in a cloud of brake-shoe smoke. Photo by Carl M. Johnson.

86

At the first curve out of Altoona, the fireman of New York–Chicago TT-1 looks back over his train from the piggybacker's lead GP9. A J1 drifts downward through the morning mist on track 1. Photo by Philip R. Hastings, 1956.

After helping train 13, the *Southwestern Mail*, to Gallitzin, K4s 3674 drops back down to Altoona. The Pacific has just passed F units in A-B-A configuration easing a freight down track 2. Photo by Fred McLeod, October 1950.

Seen from the observation car of the eastbound *Aerotrain,* J1a 6486 fights toward the Horseshoe Curve, about 1½ miles ahead. Photo by Philip R. Hastings.

Horseshoe Curve

In a shot from the signal bridge at the east end of the Horseshoe Curve, M1 6853 leads a head-end-heavy local west past Kittanning Point station, shortly before the demolition of the picturesque stone structure in 1940. Photo by H. W. Pontin, Railroad Photographic Club.

At perhaps PRR's most notable milepost, 242 miles from Broad Street Station, I1s 2-10-0 6329 fights up and around the Curve with empty hoppers and gons. Pennsy's 598 I1 "Hippos" may have been viewed as obsolete by the time the last were built in 1923, but they were at home on the heavy grades of the Pittsburgh Division. Photo by M. A. Steese, October 1946.

K4s 3671, wearing PRR's short-lived Futura-style lettering introduced in 1935, rounds the Curve with an eastbound. The track in the foreground diverged from the Main Line and followed Glen White Run to serve a coal and lumber company; it was removed around 1938. Photo by Frank Quin.

Before a small but admiring crowd, an I1s 2-10-0 and N1s 2-10-2 shove hard on a westbound's cabin car. The Santa Fe was not a type associated with the PRR: there were "only" 190 of them, two-thirds were USRA-designed class N2 types, and most worked the lines west of Pittsburgh, not the original Main Line. Photo by Frank Quin.

M1 6861 on a passenger train overtakes an eastbound freight, one of whose rear-end crewmen is enjoying the view from the platform of his N5 cabin car. Behind the trains, a westbound blasts uphill, its smoke visible above the cabin car. In another going-away view, K4s Pacifics 3733 and 1339 drift downward with the *Liberty Limited* for Washington. Both photos by H. W. Pontin, Railroad Photographic Club.

The area around the tracks is covered by cinders from the stacks of thousands of steam locomotives like this I1s climbing the Horseshoe Curve with a freight. Photo by C. E. Starr.

E8s on a special train out of Harrisburg meet E7s on the eastbound *St. Louisan* at the center of Horseshoe Curve. Photo by Al Rung.

Barely moving, J1a 6427 struggles toward the Curve with empty hoppers. Soon it will pass over the tracks in foreground. The uphill pair of tracks are white with sand dust, while the downhill two are blackened with the residue of brakeshoes pressing against wheels. Photo by Philip R. Hastings, 1956.

Alco FAs move a freight west past the modest park facilities that once greeted visitors to the Horseshoe Curve.
Photo by Elmer Treloar, June 1, 1953.

An aerial view of the Horseshoe Curve from about 1940 catches an eastbound freight dropping downgrade on track 2, with a light helper engine not far behind on track 1. Large white letters to the right of the reservoir in the center of the Curve identify its function: "City of Altoona Water Supply." PRR photo.

Three miles west of the Horseshoe Curve, three K4s Pacifics lift train 95's 25-plus cars of mail and express up the grade at Allegrippus Curve. The lead engine will cut off at Gallitzin, about 3 miles ahead, and return to Altoona. Photo by Fred McLeod, October 1950.

As he eases his train toward Allegrippus, the engineer of J1 6436 watches for anything that might disrupt his careful descent of the unforgiving east slope. Photo by Fred McLeod, November 1949.

I1sa 4494, with a long string of empty hoppers and a sister "Hippo" pushing on the rear out of view beyond Bennington Curve, nears the tunnels at Gallitzin on track 4. The Main Line split at the summit: tracks 4 and 3 passed through the adjacent Gallitzin and Allegheny tunnels, while 1 and 2 used the original, two-track New Portage tunnel. Photo by Fred McLeod, October 1950.

After turning on the loop tracks at Gallitzin, I1 Decapods in helper service exit New Portage tunnel en route to Altoona and another shove. Photo by Fred McLeod, October 1949.

Gallitzin, top of the mountain: At AR tower, helpers boost two eastbounds over the top simultaneously. Lending a hand to a mixed freight out of Pittsburgh is a Baldwin Centipede set, while EMD F3s do the honors for a coal train that entered the Main Line at Cresson. Beyond the tower are the two loop tracks and fuel and water facilities for helpers out of Altoona, and the two westbound tracks. Photo by Philip R. Hastings, 1956.

103

On a wet night, an eastbound freight waits at AR block and interlocking station, the PRR term for the facilities most roads called towers. Photo by Philip R. Hastings, 1956.

Long-nosed Alco RSD12s 8607 and 8608 leave Gallitzin tunnel shortly before the smoke erupting from Allegheny tunnel materializes into J1 6456. Both westbounds are seen from Gallitzin's Jackson Street bridge. Photos by Philip R. Hastings, 1956.

I1s 4360 rolls coal hoppers west past straw-hatted passengers at the Cresson station. The view dates from the late 1920s or early '30s — the 2-10-0 is fitted with electric headlight and classification lights but still sports a bar pilot and extended piston rods. Photo by Fred Eidenbenz.

With slide detector fences standing guard, Fairbanks-Morse H20-44s 8919 and 8929 boom eastward near Cassandra. The switcher-type carbody is deceptive, since each unit packs 2000 horsepower. Photo by Bob Lorenz, August 18, 1960.

Two Hippos give it their all as they help an eastbound through the cut near Cassandra in the late 1940s. The fellow perched on the trailing tender is most likely a brakeman.

In another view from the late '40s, two K4s waltz across a fill between Cassandra and Portage with an eastbound Railway Express extra. Both photos by Wayne Brumbaugh.

A J1 shepherds a train with a variety of high-and-wide loads eastward at South Fork. PRR's 125 Texas types were "foreigners": Though built at Altoona from 1942 to 1944, they were near duplicates of Chesapeake & Ohio's T-1 class — a wartime expediency that helped keep the Pittsburgh Division and lines west of Pittsburgh fluid under the tremendous traffic load the conflict imposed. Photo by Elmer Treloar, August 22, 1953.

Dramatically lit from behind by low winter sun, an I1s puts on a show in Staple Bend Cut about 7 miles east of Johnstown with an eastbound. Nearly obscured by the laboring Decapod's exhaust is the overhead bridge of the Conemaugh & Black Lick Railroad, a Johnstown-area switching line. Photo by Wayne Brumbaugh.

With Johnstown's 1915 brick station and high-level platforms in the background, F3s curve eastward toward 39 miles of mountain railroading. Photo by Elmer Treloar, August 22, 1953.

A trip over the mountain

In April 1948, Linn H. Westcott, then on the editorial staff of *Trains* Magazine, rode a steam-powered passenger train eastward across the Pittsburgh Division. He took several photos from the rear vestibule, paying special attention to the Johnstown-Altoona segment.

Just east of Parkhill, the east portal of Staple Bend Tunnel is visible above the Main Line. Completed for the Allegheny Portage Railroad in 1834, it was the first railroad tunnel in the U. S.

At Wilmore (upper right), the locomotive on Westcott's train scoops water on the fly, as evidenced by the water sloshing out the end of the track pan.

Halfway between Cresson and Gallitzin, state highway 53 crosses the three eastbound tracks (numbered 0, 1, and 2) as they head for the summit tunnel on a 1.53 percent grade, and descending westbound tracks 3 and 4, at the right.

Having exited New Portage tunnel and crossed the New Portage Secondary (the Muleshoe Curve line) on a bridge, Westcott's train descends the short stretch of 2.36 percent called "the slide." Tracks 3 and 4 enter Allegheny and Gallitzin tunnels; atop the ridge is the settlement of Tunnelhill.

Somewhere on the east slope (lower left), Westcott's train passes a steam engine and an F3 set shoving the rear of a freight.

PRR's Altoona station falls away to the rear as Westcott continues his eastward journey.

113

Eastbound F3s exit the short tunnel at Radebaugh, 2 miles west of Greensburg. Track 4 swings off to the left into its own tunnel. Photo by Charles McCreary, August 21, 1949.

This three-unit F3 set is about a year old as it rolls 90 cars eastward a few miles west of Johnstown. The Main Line is five tracks here; two more tracks — the Sang Hollow Extension — are over on the north bank of the Conemaugh River for the 13 miles between SG tower and Conpitt Junction. Photo by Fred McLeod, May 1949.

Though not a railroad structure, the George Westinghouse Bridge, which carried the Lincoln Highway over the Turtle Creek valley at East Pittsburgh, was the most imposing landmark on the west end of the Pittsburgh Division. E8s 5713 and 5712 lead the eastbound *Juniata* beneath the massive span and the Union Railroad truss bridge. Ahead of the units is one of Pennsy's distinctive keystone whistle signs. Photo by Ralph E. Hallock.

Just west of the Westinghouse bridge, the *Juniata* curves past U. S. Steel's Edgar Thomson Works, named for PRR's third president. Photo by Ralph E. Hallock.

Its days as a front-line freight engine long past, 38-year-old H8sa 2-8-0 7784 loafs along with a way freight (sporting an RPO at the head end) near East Liberty. The Consolidation looks well cared for, but two months later it was sold for scrap. Photo by Fred McLeod, April 4, 1948.

K4s 359 and an A-B set of E7s team up on the *Duquesne,* train 74, at East Liberty. The train stopped there only to receive passengers. Photo by W. H. N. Rossiter, July 1952.

At 28th Street Yard in downtown Pittsburgh, K4s Pacifics and T1 duplexes fill the ready tracks while a 2-8-0 switches cars. Photo by Fred McLeod, April 1948.

Beneath the trainshed that covered PRR's Pittsburgh station tracks until the postwar improvements, G5s 4-6-0 5730 is ready to head east on a commuter run, while a troop train stands on a through track at the right. The Ten-Wheeler is one of 90 PRR built for commuter service in the mid-1920s. Its train consists of P54-family coaches, unpowered versions of the MU cars that carried Philadelphia commuters. Photo by Kent W. Cochrane.

Temporary wood umbrella sheds served until Pennsy completed its massive Pittsburgh depot project in the late '50s. Photo by Linn W. Westcott, April 1948.

Alco RS3s on commuter trains and EMD switchers working the station greet the engine crew of the *Metropolitan*'s lead E unit as the train arrives at Pennsylvania Station, Pittsburgh. Photo by A. C. Kalmbach, May 1952.

In a view from the Pittsburgh station's 12-story head building, the new steel-and-glass shed takes shape over the tracks. The long building at left is PRR's new freight house, part of the improvement project. PRR photo.

The Pittsburgh station's ornate rotunda served both as a taxi stand and a gateway to the Pennsylvania's Main Line across its namesake state. Beyond the stone structure, trains curve onto the Allegheny River bridge on the line to Cleveland, Detroit, Fort Wayne, and Chicago. In the foreground, SW1 5991 shifts cars on tracks leading to Columbus, Cincinnati, Indianapolis, and St. Louis. Photo by Philip R. Hastings, 1956.

Conrail SD50 6720 and SD35 6028 lead a westbound TrailVan intermodal train past MG tower, 1½ miles above Horseshoe Curve. Interlocking towers are nearly gone from the Main Line, and MG hasn't been in regular service for years. Photo by Fred W. Frailey, March 17, 1984.

The Main Line today

Throughout the final years of the Pennsylvania Railroad and the brief Penn Central era, the Main Line saw relatively few changes, apart from reductions in passenger trains and physical plant. But the reorganization of Northeastern railroading under Conrail has had a profound impact, particularly on the Main Line's east end.

After Conrail's 1976 inception, Amtrak assumed ownership of the Philadelphia-Harrisburg segment, leaving the new carrier with the freight lines tributary to the Main Line and to Amtrak's much busier Northeast Corridor. Conrail found the passenger railroad's trackage-rights and electric-power fees to be too high, and began shifting traffic off and de-electrifying even its own ex-PRR eastern lines. Today, most New York/Philadelphia-Harrisburg freight moves via former Lehigh Valley and Reading lines. Through freights are gone from the east end of the Main Line, as are helper districts, 52nd Street yard and enginehouse, the Glen Loch-Thorndale portion of the Trenton Cutoff, and the Atglen & Susquehanna low-grade line.

Amtrak traffic has generally consisted of four or six long-haul trains and several Harrisburg runs each day. The discontinuance of the *Broadway Limited* in September 1995 left the Main Line with but two New York-Pittsburgh day trains, operating via 30th Street Station, though a resuscitated *Broadway* was scheduled to replace one of the day trains in November 1996. Amtrak has used 30th Street ever since 1980, when it quit using North Philadelphia station as the Philly stop for the remnants of the east-west fleet. These trains use diesel locomotives west of 30th Street, as do many "Keystone Service" trains for their entire Philly-Harrisburg runs.

The Paoli Local is alive and well, part of the regional commuter service run by the Southeastern Pennsylvania Transportation Authority. The Center City Commuter Rail tunnel, which linked Suburban Station with all the ex-Reading lines in 1984, has enhanced traditional Philadelphia-Paoli service on the east end. Most Paoli trains now run to and from Lansdale as SEPTA route R5. The development boom west of Paoli has seen increased service to Parkesburg.

West of Harrisburg, the Main Line is still a conduit for freight — one of Conrail's two major routes between the East and Midwest — though it's considerably leaner than in PRR days. Enola Yard, having surrendered its "world's largest" title long ago, was closed as a major classification facility by Conrail in 1994. Signal bridges — unneeded on double track — are disappearing, as are the distinctive position-light signals, which are yielding to color-light types all along the "Pittsburgh Line," as Conrail terms its Harrisburg-Pittsburgh artery. No functioning interlocking towers, once a signature element of the PRR scene, remain on the old Middle Division, which is now mostly a two-track, Centralized Traffic Controlled railroad. Sharp eyes are needed to find traces of track pans and other steam facilities, though a wide spot in the right-of-way and a scale installation mark the site of the Denholm coal wharf.

Altoona serves Conrail in the same role today as it did under PRR: system locomotive shop. The shops perform all major repairs, overhauls, and rebuildings on Conrail's diesel fleet and do a healthy business in contract work for other railroads. While locomotive design, construction, and testing are hardly the major functions at Altoona they were in steam days, the shops did assemble part of an order of SD60M diesels in 1995 when General Motors' own crowded plant couldn't meet Conrail's delivery schedule. Major freight-car work is done at Samuel Rea Shops in nearby Hollidaysburg.

Operationally, Altoona is no longer a division point — crews and locomotives run right through. Helpers for westbound trains tie on there, but are based in Cresson.

Beyond Altoona, the grades are as tough as ever, and many Conrail freights run with helpers the length of the former Pittsburgh Division, both east- and westbound. Many work just the east slope, turning on the one remaining Gallitzin loop. Three main tracks are in service between Altoona and Conpit (no longer spelled with the second "t"), with a fourth at the top of the west slope between Gallitzin and Cresson. Two tracks serve west of Conpit, leaving space for a busway on the last few miles into Pittsburgh, whose easterly commuter trains ceased in 1964. CTC came late to the 39 miles over the mountain, which boasted six active towers in the late 1980s; in mid-1996., only three remained.

In a project whose state sponsorship echoed that of the original Main Line of Public Works, Conrail and the Commonwealth of Pennsylvania jointly funded extensive work to improve clearances on CR's major cross-state lines so they could accommodate double-stack containers. Much of the $97 million budget went into the tunnels at Spruce Creek and Gallitzin. The project enlarged one of the two bores at Spruce Creek to handle two high-clearance tracks and mothballed the other for emergency use only. Similarly, Gallitzin tunnel is now held in reserve in its original state, while adjacent Allegheny tunnel now hosts two spacious tracks and New Portage, a single track. The clearance work was completed in 1995.

The Main Line's Pennsylvania Railroad heritage is kept alive at various locations. Major station buildings remain at Philadelphia (Suburban and 30th Street), Lancaster, Harrisburg, Huntingdon, Greensburg, and Pittsburgh. Local groups have restored towers at Huntingdon and Harrisburg; the latter's National Railway Historical Society chapter also cares for GG1 4859, displayed under the trainshed. At Lewistown, the Pennsylvania Railroad Technical & Historical Society is restoring the historic depot to house the group's extensive collection of PRR archives. The Altoona Railroaders Memorial Museum's collection of rolling stock stands across the Main Line from the Amtrak station and beside its new home in the former Master Mechanic's Building, once part of the shop complex. The museum also operates the visitor facilities at Horseshoe Curve, extensively upgraded from 1990 to 1992.

Index of Photographs

Locations
Allegrippus Curve: 100, 101
Altoona: 65, 77-79, 85-88, 113
Bailey: 59
Bennington Curve: cover, 4
Cassandra: 107, 108
Coatesville: 33, 34
Cresson: 106, 112
Denholm: 63, 64, 66
Downingtown: 30
Duncannon: 57, 58
East Liberty: 117, 118
East Pittsburgh: 115, 116
Enola Yard: 51-53
Gallitzin: 102-105, 113
Glen Loch: 29
Harrisburg: 36-43
Horseshoe Curve: 80, 91-99, 124
Huntingdon: 71, 72
Johnstown: 111, 114
Kittaning Point: 90
Lewistown: 44, 67-69
Mapleton: 70
Merion: 25, 26
Millerstown: 61
Newport: 60
Overbrook: 21-24
Paoli: 28
Parkhill: 112
Perdix: 54-56
Philadelphia, Broad Street: 15, 16
Philadelphia, 30th Street: 17-19
Philadelphia, Zoo: 20
Pittsburgh: 119-123
Radebaugh: 114
Rockville Bridge: 48-50
Royalton: 35
South Fork: 109
Spruce: 73
Staple Bend: 110
Thompsontown: 62
Thorndale: 31, 32
Tyrone: 74-76
Wayne: 27
Whitford: 10
Wilmore: 112

Diesel locomotives
DR-6-4-20 No. 5777: 38
DR-4-4-15 No. 9590: 55
DR-12-8-1500/2 No. 5819: 57
DR-12-8-1500/2 No. 5823: 57
DR-12-8-1500/2 No. 5827: 69
E7 No. 5846: 118
E7 No. 5862: 36
E8 No. 5707: 68
E8 No. 5712: 115
E8 No. 5713: 115
E8 No. 5805: 116
E8 No. 5839: 61
E8 No. 5709: 66
E8 No. 5809: 74
F3 No. 9515: 111
F3 No. 9521: 114
F3 No. 9545: 103
F3 No. 9552: 113
F3 No. 9794: 60
F3 No. 9817: 53
GP9 No. 7006: 53
GP9 No. 7012: 53
GP9 No. 7024: 53
H20-44 No. 8919: 107
H20-44 No. 8929: 107
RSD-12 No. 8607: 105
RSD-12 No. 8608: 105
SD50 No. 6720 (Conrail): 124
SW1 No. 5991: 123

Steam locomotives
2-8-0 No. 7784: 117
2-8-2 No. 714: 30, 52
2-10-0 No. 4360: 106
2-10-0 No. 4494: 102
2-10-0 No. 4552: 102
2-10-0 No. 4581: 93
2-10-0 No. 4594: 54
2-10-0 No. 6329: 91
2-10-2 No. 9217: 93
2-10-4 No. 6154: 80
2-10-4 No. 6436: 101
2-10-4 No. 6456: 105
2-10-4 No. 6486: 89
4-4-2 No. 645: 18
4-6-0 No. 5730: 120
4-6-2 No. 12: 72
4-6-2 No. 299: 59
4-6-2 No. 359: 118
4-6-2 No. 1339: 94
4-6-2 No. 3671: 92
4-6-2 No. 3674: 88
4-6-2 No. 3733: 94
4-6-2 No. 3820: 43
4-6-2 No. 3888: cover, 4
4-6-2 No. 5334: 43
4-6-2 No. 5347: 100
4-6-2 No. 5433: 40
4-8-2 No. 6717: 64
4-8-2 No. 6736: 56
4-8-2 No. 6743: 44
4-8-2 No. 6749: 50
4-8-2 No. 6853: 90
4-8-2 No. 6861: 94
4-8-2 No. 6888: 65
4-8-2 No. 6889: 67
4-8-2 No. 6921: 63, 64
4-8-2 No. 6979: 70
4-4-4-4 No. 5532: 79
4-4-4-4 No. 5544: 71
4-4-4-4 No. 5548: 67
4-4-4-4 No. 6110: 42

Electric locomotives
E2b No. 4942: 34
E2b No. 4944: 34
E44 No. 4411: 34
FF2 No. 6: 31
GG1 No. 4819: 24
GG1 No. 4844: 19
GG1 No. 4845: 15
GG1 No. 4858: 36
GG1 No. 4863: 35
GG1 No. 4884: 37
GG1 No. 4899: 23
P5a No. 4710: 29
P5a No. 4734: 34
P5a No. 4737: 22
P5a No. 4755: 32

Photographers
Ahrens, John P.: 44, 67
Bradley, J. E.: 37
Brown, C. A.: 30
Brumbaugh, Wayne: 108, 110
Carleton, Paul: 58
Clifford, Pier: 28
Cochrane, Kent W.: 120
Douglas, Kenneth L.: 75
Eidenbenz, Fred: 106
Ellis, Wayne P.: 18, 48, 66
Elston, Charles A.: 29
Frailey, Fred W.: 124
Fryer, Aaron G.: 20-24
Fuller, J. B.: 13
Furler, Donald W.: 59
Gay, Theo. A.: 42
Hallock, Ralph E.: 115, 116
Hastings, Philip R.: 49, 50, 51, 52, 87, 97, 103-105, 123
Hibbs, Elizabeth: 27
Hull, Ralph W.: 50
Johnson, Carl M.: 86
Kalmbach, A. C.: 121
Kern, F. R.: 55, 57
Knox, David G.: 10, 35
Lorenz, Bob: 74, 107
Maxwell, J. W.: 43
McCreary, Charles: 114
McLellan, J. A.: 25
McLeod, Fred: cover, 4, 61, 73, 80, 88, 100-102, 114, 117, 119
Pearson, Kenneth E.: 71
Pennsylvania Railroad: 15, 16, 19, 77, 99, 122
Pennypacker, Bert: 32, 33, 36
Pontin, H. W.: 90, 94
Price, William P.: 72
Quin, Frank: 92, 93
Rossiter, W. H. N.: 118
Rung, Al: 38, 40, 41, 78, 79, 96
Short, Richard S.: 26
Starr, C. E.: 95
Steese, M. A.: 91
Tatnall, Frank: 34
Treloar, Elmer: 98, 109, 111
Weaver, Clarence R.: 69
Westcott, Linn H.: 39, 85, 112, 113, 121
Wood, Don: 31, 53, 54, 56, 60, 62-65, 68, 70, 76

Named passenger trains
Admiral: 10
Aerotrain: 58
Broadway Limited: 26, 78
Cincinnati Limited: 79
Duquesne: 35, 59, 118
Juniata: 49, 115, 116
Manhattan Limited: 61
Pennsylvania Limited: 37
Susquehannock: 32
St. Louisan: 36, 66, 74, 96
Trail Blazer: 38